P9-DNK-489

This book belongs to:

....

who will
always
be adored

I love you like:

....

I Love You Like Sunshine

How everyday play and bedtime stories grow love,
connections, and brainpower

Mariana Glusman, MD, and Marta Killner, MD

West Walker Publishing House, Chicago

West Walker Publishing House

Any questions may be addressed to 4043 N. Avers Ave. Chicago, IL, 60618
westwalkerpublishers@gmail.com; iloveyoulikesubshine.com

No part of this publication may be reproduced in any form, by any means,
without the written permission of the publisher

ISBN-10: 0-692-63285-9
ISBN-13: 978-0-692-63285-7

Text and photographs copyright © 2016 by Mariana Glusman and Marta Killner
All rights reserved

Library of Congress Control Number: 2016902407

Design by Jennifer McLaughlin

Printed in the U.S.A by Vision Integrated Graphics Group LLC
Second printing August 2016

Dedication

To Doug, my biggest supporter and best friend
I love you like sunshine and butter, but not at the same time!

To Abby, James, and Lizzy
You are the best teachers a pediatrician could ask for. I'm so proud to be your mom.

To my mother, father, and siblings
3 countries, 2 languages, 13 houses, endless love and support.
Home is where we are.

To my patients
Thank you for letting me be a part of your lives.

To Alex, I miss you.

—MG

To Silvio, my partner in adventures, for 54 years of steadfast love and support.

To my children and grandchildren who never cease to amaze me.

To my parents, who taught me to love words.

To my daughter, friend, fellow-pediatrician and co-author, a gifted teacher and healer from the start,
an inspired mentor and tireless advocate for children, with love and admiration.

—MK

Introduction

At first it may seem hard to believe that they actually sent you home with this baby. If you feel that way, you are not alone.

In my 20 years as a pediatrician, I've heard hundreds of parents joke about needing a parenting manual. Their usual worries about eating, peeing, pooping, rashes, sneezing, and so on are easy for a pediatrician to handle. But many of the questions underlying those practical concerns are not as simple: "How will I be as a parent? How can I prepare my baby for the challenges we all face? What if I mess up?"

I had those same questions when I brought my first daughter home from the hospital 23 years ago. Abby was six months old when I finished medical school and started my training to become a pediatrician. I learned how to be a doctor at the same time I that I learned how to be a mother, so I know the advice doctors give families is not always easy to follow. It can be hard to think straight when you're worried and sleep-deprived.

As I studied child development, I proudly watched Abby achieve each of her own milestones. I started reading to her when she was a little baby, though I had not yet learned that reading aloud is one of the most important things that parents can do to help their children succeed. I read to her because she loved it, and because lying in bed with her felt so sweet and soothing after those punishingly long shifts at the hospital. When she became a toddler, if I was too tired to read, we'd play Sleeping Beauty: I would pretend to prick my finger and fall asleep while Abby, as the prince, would sing a song and then kiss me so I'd wake up . . . for just long enough to prick my finger and close my eyes again!

At work I expected the babies and toddlers I saw to be developing just as mine was, and sometimes they were. But by the time Abby was about 18 months old, it was clear that many of my patients were lagging behind her in some areas, especially in their language and cognitive skills. I also noticed that not many of them had families who routinely read aloud with them.

Toward the end of my pediatric training, in 1996, I learned about Reach Out and Read (ROR), a program being developed by doctors in Boston to promote literacy. During regular checkups, from six months to five years, pediatricians with ROR gave books to their patients and talked with families about the importance of reading to young children. The results were encouraging and confirmed my own observations as a mom. I was hooked.

In 2001, I started a ROR site at the clinic in Chicago's Uptown neighborhood, where I still work. Since then, I have become the medical director of Reach Out and Read Illinois, which helps support 130 sites throughout the state. I am also involved in several national ROR initiatives.

Over the past 25 years, Reach Out and Read has expanded to more than 5,000 clinics in the U.S. and has become one of the most important interventions primary care pediatricians can offer their patients. More than 15 peer-reviewed articles demonstrate that ROR significantly improves children's language development and school readiness. Each year we distribute more than six million books to young patients.

I like to think of those books as vaccines against illiteracy.

At the same time, there has been an explosion in our understanding of how babies learn and how their brains develop. We have known for a long time that the more children see and hear the better they learn. For instance, it's been shown that young children who hear more words than their peers develop more advanced vocabularies.

But now we realize that kids don't just absorb language like sponges. They need to be active in their learning. Back-and-forth communication between babies and their caregivers, also known as "serve-and-return" interaction, is crucial in reinforcing the brain pathways involved in language and cognitive development. For that reason, in 2014 the American Academy of Pediatrics started recommending that pediatricians teach caregivers to talk, sing, and read with children beginning at birth.

From my experience with ROR, I knew of many great books to give to babies starting at six months. But this new AAP recommendation made me wonder about what the best books for newborns might be. It's not easy to read with newborns because their responses are so subtle. They don't coo or babble or reach for things—or even smile. You really have to pay attention to catch their responses.

That is why I wrote this book.

I Love You Like Sunshine will help you recognize your newborn's subtle cues and give you specific tips to encourage the serve-and-return interactions that will promote your baby's brain development. I recruited my mother, a photographer and retired pediatrician, to take pictures of babies and parents to illustrate the joy that comes from interacting this way. I think you'll agree that her photos really capture the beauty and intensity of relationships between babies and those who love them.

I Love You Like Sunshine is two books in one, a book for babies and a book for parents. It's a book to read aloud to your infant, who will look at the baby pictures with fascination and delight and will hear in the rhymes the sounds that make up words. But the real reason your baby will love it (and other baby books, too) is that she loves to listen to your voice. The more you read the book, the more your baby will learn to recognize and enjoy it. Notice how her reactions to the book change as she gets older. Like everything else about infants, even a week can make a huge difference.

This is also a book for parents. In the margins and at the end of the book you will find advice based on knowledge I've gathered during two decades as both a pediatrician and a mom. You can use my hints on "things to know," "things to try," and "things to notice" while reading aloud and also during your daily routine.

On the final pages I've included information about brain development that's central to my recommendations. Babies are strong and resilient but, in addition to nutrition and safety, they need lots of love and attention to thrive. You don't need expensive gadgets to enrich your baby's environment, and it shouldn't be difficult or stressful. All you have to do is talk, sing, read, cuddle, and play together as much as possible.

I hope you enjoy this book, too. My goals are simply to help you relax and enjoy being with your newborn, and to provide you with information and practices that will help your baby develop and reach toward her potential.

It gets easier with time, and each new phase will be a rewarding learning process for your baby and for you. Have fun!

—Mariana Glusman, MD
2016

DID YOU KNOW?

Babies love to look at baby faces, and they love to hear your voice.

THINGS TO TRY

You can point to the picture on the next page. "Where are the baby's hands? Here they are! Where are your hands? Lets count your fingers. 1, 2, 3 . . ." You can also point out your baby's body parts at other times, such as during feeding, baths, and diaper changes. Experiment with different ways to tell your baby how much you love him. "I love you like sunshine," "I love you like a big juicy peach," "I love you like hot cocoa on a cold day," "I love you like . . ."

THINGS TO NOTICE

What's the most amazing thing you notice when you look at your baby?

I look at you when you're asleep,
I can't believe you're here.

Your tiny nails, your lovely lips,
Your precious curving ears.

I look at you when you're awake,
And you look back at me!

I read you books and point things out—
So much for you to see!

DID YOU KNOW?

Many people think newborn babies can't see. That's not true. They can see a lot, especially close up.

THINGS TO TRY

Read with your baby and tell her about the pictures in the books. What is interesting about them? Read the books you remember from when you were little. (Were they nursery rhymes? Fairy tales?). Read anything that interests you. Read what makes you happy!

THINGS TO NOTICE

How does your baby react when you read with her? Does she briefly look at the pictures? Does she look at you? Although she may not seem interested at first, the more you read with her the more she will respond.

DID YOU KNOW?

You can't spoil a baby!
Your baby needs to know
that you will come when
he needs you. The closer
you listen the easier it is
to tell his cries apart.

THINGS TO TRY

Every baby responds
differently to different
ways of being soothed.
Many babies like to be
swaddled and gently
rocked. Ask your baby
what's wrong and why
he's crying. "Are you
hungry? Are you tired?"
Although he won't answer
in words he will start to
give you cues and
your responses will
show him that you are
always there for him.

THINGS TO NOTICE

How does your baby
like to be soothed?
How does he let you
know what he needs?

You have different cries and sounds
you make to tell me you're upset.

I pick you up and hold you close
And you relax into my chest.

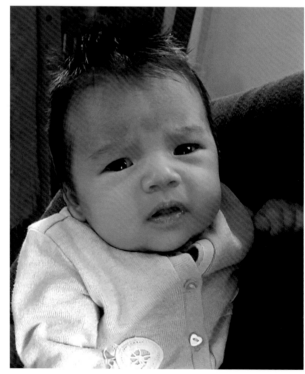

Your expressions, ever changing,
Show all feelings in one place.

Curious, glad, surprised, and puzzled
Pass like clouds across your face.

DID YOU KNOW?

Babies usually begin smiling on purpose at around four weeks. But even before that your baby will flash you a smile here and there. There are few things more rewarding than seeing your baby smile.

THINGS TO TRY

Name the expressions you notice on her face. If she frowns, ask her if she's upset. If she happens to smile, you can mention how beautiful that smile is, or you can ask her what's so funny!

THINGS TO NOTICE

Do your baby's expressions change when you talk with her? How does she respond to other people?

DID YOU KNOW?

Babies love music. They can even recognize music that they heard in the womb. Listening to poems that rhyme helps babies learn the sounds that make up words, like c-a-t, and m-a-t. This is very important when they start learning to read.

THINGS TO TRY

Sing a lullaby. What songs do you remember from your childhood? The "Itsy Bitsy Spider"? The ABC song? "Row, Row, Row Your Boat"? What are your favorite songs now? Look for children's poetry books and rhyming stories to share with your baby. Emphasize the rhymes as you read them aloud.

THINGS TO NOTICE

How does your baby react when you sing? Are there songs he seems to like better than others? What does he do when you play music? Does he move more? Does he make sounds?

There's so much I want to show you
And teach you about the world.

I sing to you and play with you
And fill your day with words.

I tell you stories and you listen.
You turn when you hear a noise.

You're not even a month old yet,
And you recognize my voice!

DID YOU KNOW?

Babies learn to recognize familiar voices during the first few weeks of life. They may even know their mother's voice at birth.

THINGS TO TRY

Notice what seems interesting to your baby and talk about it. Is it the lights in the ceiling? His hands? A shadow on the wall? Name and describe the things you see. What color are they? Are they big or small? Are they soft or hard? Are they near or far? Tell your own stories. What were things like when you were little?

THINGS TO NOTICE

Does your baby seem to recognize your voice? What about those of other family members?

DID YOU KNOW?

It's not always easy to talk with a newborn. Sometimes you may feel like you are going a little crazy!

THINGS TO TRY

When your baby makes sounds, respond as if he told you something. Taking turns vocalizing back and forth is the way babies learn to talk. Remember that babies learn by interacting with the people around them. TVs, tablets, and phones can distract kids but they can't respond to your baby's cues the way you do.

THINGS TO NOTICE

Does your baby listen when you talk and coo when you stop? Does it begin to feel like you're having a conversation with him?

We take turns cooing and talking,
And you really get excited.

We have long conversations,
Though they often feel one-sided!

I'm really tired, I won't lie,
And I'm sometimes lonely, too.

I get sad and want to cry,
But I feel better holding you.

DID YOU KNOW?

At times, caring for a baby can make you feel sad or lonely. Having a newborn is exhausting and sometimes frustrating. It can also be a little scary. It's normal to worry.

THINGS TO TRY

If you can, take a little time for yourself, and rest when the baby sleeps. It's OK to ask for help. Although they may not show it, other parents feel the same way you do. Talk with your pediatrician or your OB if you feel overwhelmed or depressed.

THINGS TO NOTICE

How are you feeling? Are you happy? Do you feel like crying? Both? Who can help when you need a break?

DID YOU KNOW?

Repetition and routines are very important as babies learn to make sense of the world around them.

THINGS TO TRY

Make reading aloud with your baby a part of your routine during naptime, bedtime, or whatever time works for your family. Have fun, be silly, make jokes. Maybe you're the only one who thinks they're funny and that's OK! Dance around, sing your favorite songs, cuddle. It not only feels good, it's good for your baby.

THINGS TO NOTICE

How do you feel when you talk and sing and read and play with your baby? Are you becoming more confident as the days go by?

FINAL NOTE

I hope you and your baby enjoy this book and keep reading it, along with other baby books. Most of all, I wish you and your family millions of shared moments of joy, discovery, and love.

My sweet sunshine I adore you,
And I promise from the start,

That I'll talk and sing and read and play
And love you with all my heart!

ADVICE FOR PARENTS

TUMMY TIME

- When babies are awake they should be on their tummy as much as possible. This helps their arms and neck get strong, and keeps their head from getting flat on the back.

SOME POINTS ABOUT SAFETY

- Your baby should always ride in a car seat. Make sure that it is correctly set up, in the back seat, facing the rear window.
- Be sure you have smoke and carbon monoxide detectors installed in your home.
- Do not smoke or let anyone smoke near your baby. Even the smoke particles left behind on clothing or furniture or in cars after someone smokes can be harmful to babies.

SKIN AND THINGS

- Newborns very commonly get rashes on their face, body, and diaper area. Most rashes are not serious and go away by themselves, but check with your baby's doctor if you have concerns.
- Barrier creams, such as zinc oxide, A&D Ointment, or Desitin, can help prevent diaper rashes.
- At about one week of age, most babies' skin peels. There is no need to put on lotions for this.
- Your baby's belly button stump should fall out between one and three weeks of age. Call your baby's doctor if there is redness around the belly button or an unpleasant smell.
- Baby girls can sometimes have vaginal discharge which can even have a little blood in it. That's due to your hormones. This goes away in about a week.
- Circumcisions heal in about a week. At first the tip of the penis looks very red and then it turns purplish gray. While it heals, cover the penis with Vaseline and gauze so the skin does not stick to the diaper.

SLEEPING

- Newborns need between 16-18 hours of sleep a day, though some need more and some need less than that. They usually sleep 2 or 3 hours at a time and wake up multiple times at night. Rest when you can.
- When not sleeping they should be alert and looking around.
- Babies should always be put on their back to sleep. This cuts back on the risk of Sudden Infant Death Syndrome or "crib death."
- Make sure there are no pillows, bumpers, or heavy blankets in the crib or bassinet.

PEEING AND POOPING

• By the time babies are 3 or 4 days old (once the breast milk has come in for breast-fed babies, but sooner with bottle-fed babies) they should be peeing at least 4 or 5 times per day. That is one wet diaper every 4-6 hours. Not enough diapers means your baby needs to feed more.

• Some babies poop every time they eat, some babies may go a few days without pooping. As long as your baby is still alert, eating and peeing well, not having hard stools, and not vomiting there is no need to worry.

EATING

• Babies typically eat every 2 or 3 hours. As they get a little older the time between feeds stretches out.

• Breast-fed babies eat 8-10 times per day, for about 15 minutes on each breast.

• Breast-feeding is natural, but it does not come naturally. It is a learning process for both moms and babies that can take a few weeks to master. Pediatricians, nurses, and lactation consultants can help.

• Bottle-fed babies typically drink 2 ounces every 2 hours or 3 ounces every 3 hours, approximately 20-24 ounces per day.

• The way to tell if your baby is eating enough is if she's gaining enough weight and peeing and pooping normally. Your pediatrician will be checking.

• Newborn babies don't need water.

ODDS AND ENDS

• It's normal for babies to spit up but frequent burping and avoiding overfeeding helps.

• Babies twitch, hiccup, sniffle, and make noises when they eat. These are typically not things to be concerned about as long as your baby doesn't have a fever and is not having a hard time breathing, breathing fast, shaking nonstop, or eating poorly.

• TV, social media, and electronics are great ways for adults to wind down and relax. However, when your baby is awake, try to keep electronics to a minimum. Studies show that caregivers interact less with their babies when the TV is on, even when it's in a different room.

WHEN TO CALL YOUR DOCTOR

• If your baby is very fussy and difficult to calm down.

• If your baby does not have awake and alert periods between naps.

• If you have concerns about your baby's eating or weight gain.

• If your baby is not peeing at least once every 6 hours.

• If your baby has not pooped in a few days and is irritable and vomiting or spitting up more than normal.

• If your baby's rectal temperature is over 100 degrees. To check you baby's rectal temperature, gently put the tip of the thermometer just inside his anus. It does not hurt. The thermometer is much smaller than a poop!

• If you have any concerns. THERE ARE NO DUMB QUESTIONS!

Building Babies' Brainpower

Singing, playing, reading responsively, and having conversations with your infant are the most effective ways to help develop your baby's brain. Here's why:

Babies are born with about 100 billion nerve cells in their brains, called neurons. Unlike cells in other parts of the body, neurons don't grow by multiplying. Instead, our brain develops when connections, also known as synapses, are made between the neurons. These connections form pathways and networks that transmit information to different parts of the brain and the body, similar to the way cable networks connect computers.

In the first few years of life, our brain goes into overdrive, making about 700 new connections per second, but after that, the number of synapses is pared down. So when you were a toddler you had about twice the number of synapses than you do now.

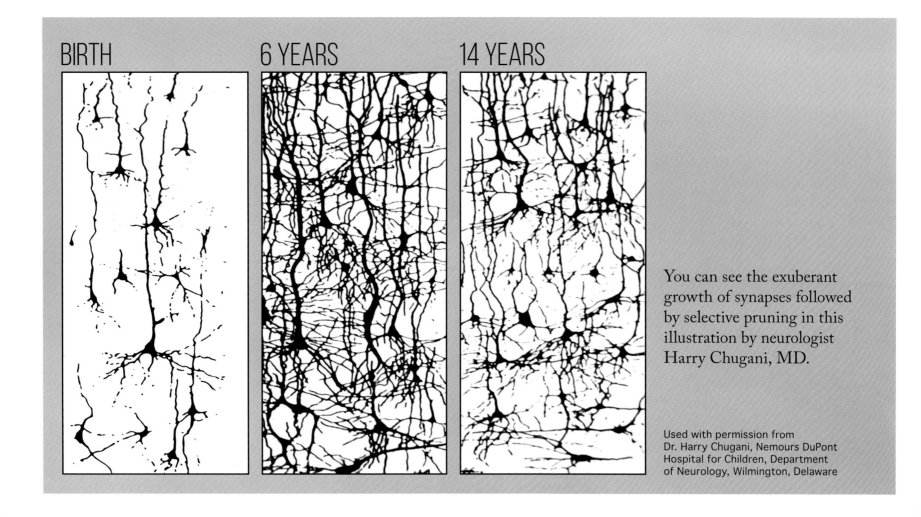

BIRTH 6 YEARS 14 YEARS

You can see the exuberant growth of synapses followed by selective pruning in this illustration by neurologist Harry Chugani, MD.

Used with permission from Dr. Harry Chugani, Nemours DuPont Hospital for Children, Department of Neurology, Wilmington, Delaware

What determines which synapses stay and which are pruned? As in many other aspects of life, the connections that remain are the ones that are reinforced. In other words, if you don't use them you lose them.

For example, young babies are able to hear and make the sounds of all languages, but as they get older they lose this ability and are only able to hear and make the sounds of the languages they grow up with. That's why most people who learn a foreign language as adults speak with an accent.

It's not just exposure that matters, however. Although we commonly say that babies are like sponges, they don't really passively absorb information. They need to be participants in their own learning, actively drawing attention from their caregivers and thriving on the mutual interaction. That's why educational videos and electronic games on their own aren't enough to encourage language or cognitive development.

The bottom line is that experience shapes brain architecture, and serve-and-return interactions with caregivers form the basis for babies' brain development. As Dr. Dana Suskind, a researcher and expert on early language development says, "Babies are not born smart, they are made smart."

Parents have the power to help their children grow to the best of their abilities. And the beautiful thing is that it's easy and fun!

About the Author

Mariana Glusman, MD, has more than two decades of experience as a pediatrician and a mom. She is an associate professor of pediatrics at Northwestern University and a primary care pediatrician at Lurie Children's Uptown Clinic, an academic community health center.

Dr. Glusman was born in Argentina and lived in Mexico until she was 11, when she moved with her family to Boston. She completed her undergraduate studies at Brown University, medical school at the University of Chicago, and her pediatric residency at Children's Memorial, now Ann and Robert H. Lurie Children's Hospital of Chicago. Dr. Glusman is an expert in language and literacy promotion in pediatrics, and has been involved with Reach Out and Read since 2001. She is the medical director of ROR Illinois, and spearheaded ROR's Leyendo Juntos (Reading Together) initiative to improve the program's impact in the Latino community. She is also involved in ROR's initiative to start literacy promotion at birth.

Dr. Glusman lives in Chicago with her high school sweetheart and two book-loving teens. Her oldest daughter, Abby, is a Preschool teacher, working on her master's in early education.

About the Photographer

Marta Killner, MD, is a retired physician turned writer and photographer after 41 years of practicing and teaching pediatrics in Mexico City, Boston, and Chicago.

Acknowledgments

I would like to thank the five families that allowed us to photograph their precious babies, Peter, Amaya, Braelyn, Jasmeena, and John. I was bowled over by how lively and expressive they were. Seeing them through their parents' loving gaze was a profoundly moving experience for which I will be eternally grateful. I am grateful as well to Alison True for her editing and for her friendship. I would also like to acknowledge my friend Sharon Weingarten, one of the most thoughtful people I know. I learned a tremendous amount from our work together. Thanks to Jennifer McLaughlin for the excellent book design and layout. Her talent and patience have been invaluable. And thanks as well to Eric Wagner for his help with the printing process.

———————◆———————

Finally, I am indebted to Reach Out and Read. Every year that I've worked with this program I've become more passionate about its mission to promote literacy as part of pediatric care. I cannot imagine walking in to do a checkup now without a book in my hand. I am incredibly grateful to ROR for the opportunities to learn, teach, coordinate, organize, and grow, but most of all for allowing me the privilege of helping improve children's lives.

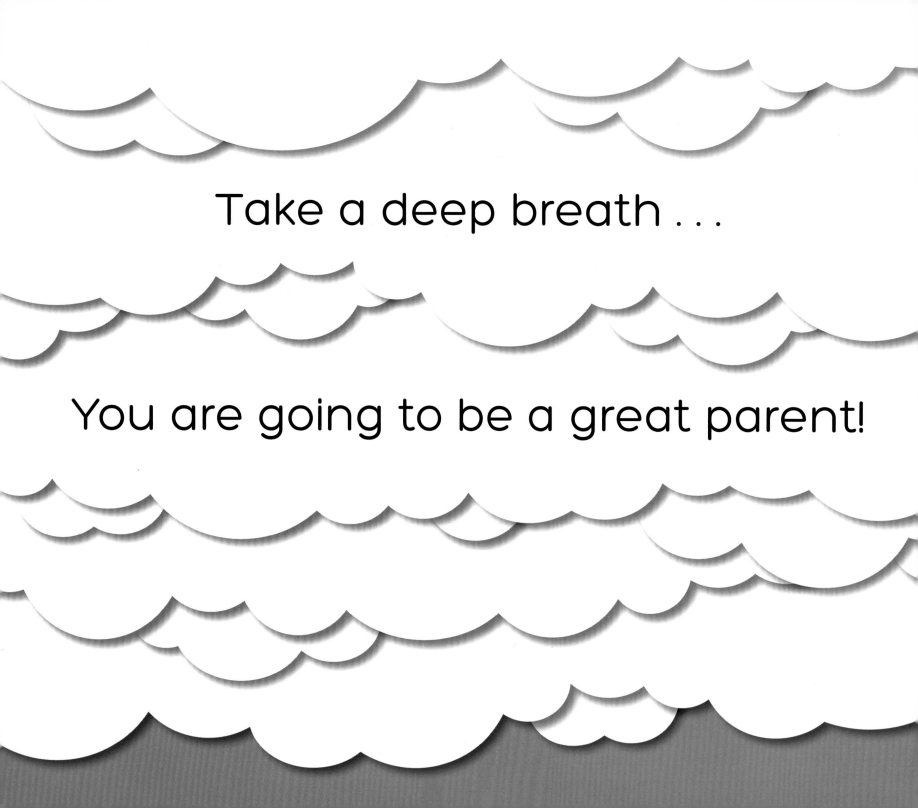